Comments on the original Theo

As a music teacher, I have all my childre
little book. The basics of music theory are laid out succinctly and
clearly, with accompanying short exercises.

Dr T J Worrall

I'm a music teacher, and can honestly say this series of books is by far
the most concise and fun to work with when helping kids. Adults also
enjoy them.

C J Gascoine

Very thorough and approachable theory practice book for young
students age 7 upwards.

Susan A. Harris

Theory can be a barrier for some young students but this book is set out
well, it's easy to read and understand, and has logical progression.
Highly recommended.

Steve Riches

I might at last be able to learn my theory and I am an old age pensioner
learning to play the piano.

Violet

Very good book that puts things very simply. I was recommended this
by my piano teacher even though I am an adult learner as it covers all
the technical points very progressively.

Amazon Customer

Music Theory is Fun Book 1

978-1-987926-09-5

Treble clef, bass clef, notes and letter names. Time names and values. Dotted notes, tied notes and rests. Accidentals, tones and semitones. Key signatures and scales (C, G, D & F major). Degrees of the scale, intervals and tonic triads. Time signatures and bar-lines. Writing music and answering rhythms. Puzzles, quizzes and ten one-page tests. Musical terms dictionary and list of signs.

Music Theory is Fun Book 2

978-1-987926-10-1

Major key signatures to 3 sharps & flats. Minor keys to 1 sharp & flat. Degrees of the scale and intervals. Tonic triads. Keyboard, tones and semitones. Time signatures. Grouping notes and rests, triplets. Two ledger lines below and above the staves. Writing four-bar rhythms. Puzzles, quizzes and ten one-page tests. Musical terms and signs.

Music Theory is Fun Book 3

978-1-987926-11-8

Major & minor key signatures 4 sharps or flats. Harmonic and melodic minor scales. Degrees of the scale, intervals, tonic triads. Simple and compound time signatures. Grouping notes & rests. Transposition at the octave. More than two ledger lines. Writing four-bar rhythms, anacrusis. Phrases. Puzzles, quizzes and ten one-page tests. Musical terms & signs.

Music Theory is Fun Book 4

978-1-987926-12-5

Key signatures to 5 sharps or flats. Alto clef. Chromatic scale, double sharps & flats. Technical names of notes in the diatonic scale. Simple & compound time, duple, triple, quadruple. Primary triads, tonic, subdominant & dominant. Diatonic intervals up to an octave. Ornaments. Four-bar rhythms and rhythms to words. Orchestral instruments and their clefs. Puzzles, quizzes and ten one-page tests. Musical terms & signs including French.

Music Theory is Fun Book 5

978-1-987926-13-2

Key signatures to 7 sharps or flats. Tenor clef and scales. Compound intervals: major, minor, perfect, diminished & augmented. Irregular time signatures, quintuple & septuple. Tonic, super-tonic, subdominant & dominant chords. Writing at concert pitch. Short & open score. Orchestral instruments. Composing a melody. Perfect, imperfect & plagal cadences. Puzzles, quizzes and ten one-page tests. Musical terms and signs including French and German.

Music Theory is Fun – A Handy Reference

978-1-987926-14-9

A concise reference to all the rudiments of music covered by the above five Music Theory is Fun books.

MUSIC THEORY IS FUN
BOOK 4

Maureen Cox

All enquiries regarding this paperback edition to:

Mimast Inc
email: mimast.inc@gmail.com

For my son Steve

* * * * * *

If you want to play an instrument, sing well or just improve your listening, you need to read music and understand theory.

This book takes you through the theory of music in a simple, straightforward way. There are plenty of fun illustrations and a variety of activities to help you along.

Towards the back of the book there are puzzles, quizzes and ten one-page tests composed of questions you could meet in an exam. At the end of the book there is a dictionary of musical terms and a list of signs for easy reference

With my help you can continue on the road to mastering and enjoying the theory of music. With this book you can discover that Theory is Fun.

Maureen Cox

Acknowledgements

I am grateful to the many Professional Private Music Teachers and Members of the Incorporated Society of Musicians who used Theory is Fun with their pupils and to Christina Bourne, Brenda Harris, Alison Hogg, Judith Holmes, Ann Leggett and Marion Martin for their helpful suggestions. I am especially grateful to Alison Hounsome for her insightful comments and helpful recommendations in the preparation of this revised edition.

A word about this revised edition

Using the previous editions of my Theory is Fun books, more than a half million people, young and not so young, mostly in the UK, had fun learning music theory. This edition has been revised and extended to include students in other countries such as America and Canada where, for example, a bar is a measure, a minim is a half note and a tone is a whole step. Common alternatives terms are listed at the back of the book with a dictionary of musical terms and signs.

This book covers the basic rudiments of theory required by the various Boards and Colleges including the Associated Board of the Royal Schools of Music, Trinity College London, the Music Examinations Boards of Australia and New Zealand and the Royal Conservatory of Canada.

Any errors are entirely my responsibility. Should there be any in this edition, I would be most grateful for them to be drawn to my attention so that they may be corrected in a future edition.

Maureen Cox

CONTENTS

KEY SIGNATURES

In Music Theory is Fun Book 3 you learned the major and minor key signatures up to and including 4 sharps and 4 flats. You should know the minor scales in their harmonic and melodic forms.

In this book we meet the key signatures with 5 sharps and 5 flats.

Important

The A♯ is placed in the bottom space in the bass, not on the top line. If it were placed an octave higher, then in the treble clef the A♯ would be on a ledger line!

Don't forget. It's important.

Major and minor key signatures

major	key signature						minor
C	no sharps or flats						A
G			F♯				E
D		F♯		C♯			B
A		F♯	C♯		G♯		F♯
E	F♯	C♯	G♯	D♯			C♯
B	F♯	C♯	G♯	D♯	A♯		G♯
F			B♭				D
B♭		B♭		E♭			G
E♭		B♭	E♭		A♭		C
A♭	B♭	E♭	A♭	D♭			F
D♭	B♭	E♭	A♭	D♭	G♭		B♭

When you are ready to test yourself on these key signatures, turn over to page 8.

Test yourself

Name these ten keys.

___ major

___ major

___ minor

___ minor

___ major

___ major

___ minor

___ minor

___ minor

___ minor

Check your answers

10

8

THE ALTO CLEF

The alto clef is also known as the C clef. This is because middle C is found on the middle line of the stave.

It is printed like this.

If you wish, you may write it in other ways.

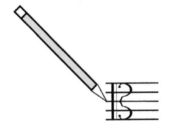

The important thing is that the two curved halves of the clef should be drawn either side of the middle line of the stave.

In former times the alto clef was found a great deal in vocal music. Nowadays the alto clef is used mainly for the viola.

Test yourself

Name these notes.

Write these key signatures in the alto clef.

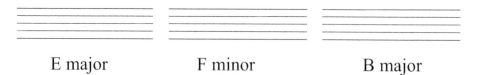

E major   F minor   B major

Rewrite the following treble clef passages in the alto clef, keeping the same pitch.

SCALES

Now you are using my Music Theory is Fun Book 4, I shall assume that you understand the differences between the harmonic and melodic minor scales.

The major key with five sharps is _____

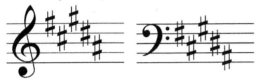

G♯ minor, the new scale in this book, also has five sharps. Its seventh note has a sharp. To raise the seventh note in minor scales you have to use a 'double sharp.'

The double sharp ✕

A double sharp raises a note one tone or whole step.

Here are the scales of G♯ minor to remind you of the differences between the harmonic and melodic minors.

Harmonic ascending

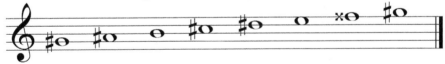

Melodic ascending

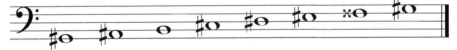

Melodic descending

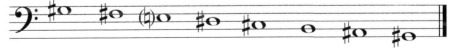

Turn to the next page when you are ready for a test.

Test yourself

Write with key signature in the treble clef the scale of D♭ major ascending and descending in minims / *half notes*. Mark the semitones / *half steps* with ⌐¬.

Write with key signature in the bass clef the scale of G♯ harmonic minor ascending and descending in semibreves / *whole notes*. Mark the semitones / *half steps* with ⌐¬.

Write without key signature in the treble clef the scale of G♯ melodic minor ascending and descending in semibreves / *whole notes*. Mark the semitones / *half steps* with ⌐¬.

Check your scales test. You might have made a small mistake which you have not noticed.

The Double Flat 𝄫

Now that you have mastered the double sharp, I shall introduce you to the double flat. When placed in front of a note, it simply lowers that note one tone / *a whole step*.

12

TECHNICAL NAMES

Each note of the scale has a different **technical** name. You have already met the **tonic** - the first note. Each note is also given a **Roman numeral**.

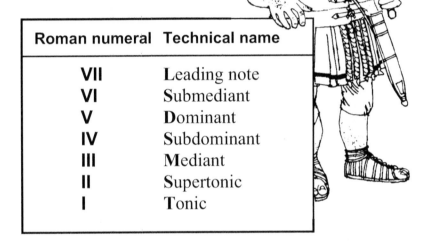

Roman numeral	Technical name
VII	Leading note
VI	Submediant
V	Dominant
IV	Subdominant
III	Mediant
II	Supertonic
I	Tonic

How can you remember these? One way is to make up a sentence. For example:

Two **S**peedy **M**otorists **S**low **D**own **S**eeing **L**ights

Now you make up a sentence.

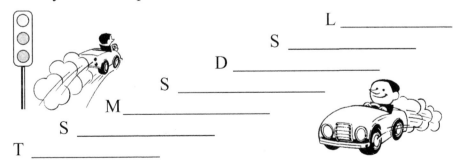

L _____

S _____

D _____

S _____

M_____

S _____

T _____

In exams you are often asked to give the technical names of notes in a short passage. Decide on the key and write out the scale. Let's say that the passage is in F harmonic minor.

Test yourself

Give the technical names of the notes (a) to (f) in the following passage. The key is D♭ major.

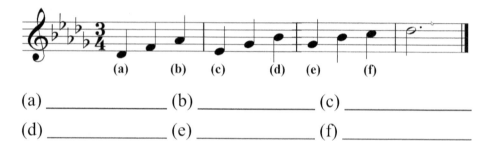

(a) _____ (b) _____ (c) _____

(d) _____ (e) _____ (f) _____

Name the key of this passage and write the technical names of the notes (a) to (f).

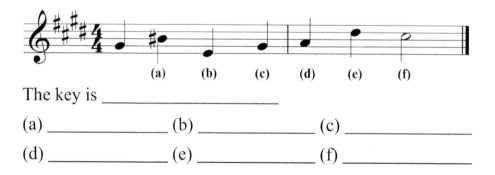

The key is _____

(a) _____ (b) _____ (c) _____

(d) _____ (e) _____ (f) _____

CHROMATIC SCALES

A chromatic scale is composed entirely of semitones / *half steps* in which a note may appear twice but never three times.

You could be asked to write a chromatic scale with or without key signature, in the treble, bass or alto clef, ascending, descending or both.

Without key signature

1. Put at least one note but not more than two notes on each line and in each space.
2. Usually use sharps ascending and flats descending.

With key signature

There is more than one way to write the scale **with** a key signature. Here is an example.

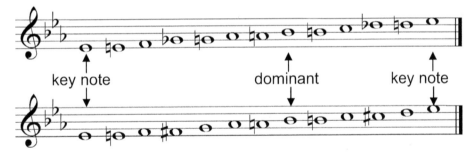

key note   dominant   key note

1. Put the key note at both ends of the scale.
2. Write the dominant **once only**.
3. Do **not** change the key note or the dominant note.
4. Do **not** put more than **two** notes on all the other lines and in all the other spaces.

Test yourself

Write one octave of a chromatic scale, in semibreves / *whole notes*, beginning on the key note or tonic

without a key signature, ascending

without a key signature, descending

with a key signature for C minor, ascending

with a key signature for G♯ minor, descending

Checking your answers?

Yes. I always do.

16

TIME SIGNATURES

$\frac{4}{8}$ is the only new simple time signature in this book. Students are sometimes confused between $\frac{2}{4}$ and $\frac{4}{8}$ time. There is no difference in notation between pieces written in $\frac{2}{4}$ and $\frac{4}{8}$. The difference is in how they are played. In $\frac{2}{4}$ time the composer wants two beats in the bar. In $\frac{4}{8}$ time the piece should have four beats in the bar.

Here is a quick reminder of simple time signatures.

duple $\frac{2}{4}$ $\frac{2}{2}$ or ¢   triple $\frac{3}{8}$ $\frac{3}{4}$ $\frac{3}{2}$ quadruple $\frac{4}{8}$ $\frac{4}{4}$ or c $\frac{4}{2}$

Duplets

In simple time you met the triplet which divided a simple beat into 3 equal parts. Now you will meet the duplet. It is found in compound time when a dotted beat is divided into 2 equal parts.

There are two ways of writing the duplet.

using dotted notes	using a ² above the pair of notes
O· = ♩·♩·	O· = ♩ ♩
♩· = ♪·♪·	♩· = ♪ ♪
♩· = ♫♪·	♩· = ♫
♪· = ♬♪·	♪· = ♬

17

Double dots

a single dot after a note lengthens it by half	the second dot is worth half the first dot
𝅗𝅥· = 𝅗𝅥 + ♩	𝅗𝅥·· = 𝅗𝅥 + ♩ + ♪
♩· = ♩ + ♪	♩·· = ♩ + ♪ + ♬

Try these:

 𝅝·· = ___ + ___ + ___

 ♪·· = ___ + ___ + ___

Add the missing bar lines to the following:

Here are some new compound time signatures. You will not find them difficult because you mastered the principles of compound time in Music Theory is Fun Book 3.

You will remember $\frac{6}{8}$ time. 6 quavers / *6 eighth notes* in a bar gave 2 dotted crotchet / *2 dotted quarter note* beats. This is compound duple time. Now we meet compound triple time with 3 dotted crotchet / *3 dotted quarter note* beats in a bar and compound quadruple time with 4 dotted crotchet / *4 dotted quarter note* beats in a bar.

Compound duple time

Compound triple time

Compound quadruple time

Grouping notes and rests

Study again pages 27 to 32 in my Music Theory is Fun
Book 3 to revise the rules for the grouping of notes and rests.

The only difference with the compound times in this book is
that the note values are doubled for $\frac{6}{4}$, $\frac{9}{4}$ and $\frac{12}{4}$ (crotchets /
quarter notes instead of quavers / *8th notes*) and halved for
$\frac{6}{16}$, $\frac{9}{16}$ and $\frac{12}{16}$ (semiquavers / *16th notes* instead of quavers /
8th notes).

The breve / *double whole note*

We have already met the breve / *double whole note* rest in
Book 3. This is what it looks like.

It is used to show a whole bar's rest in $\frac{4}{2}$ time. Written as a
note it looks like this ‖O‖. It is worth two semibreves / *two
whole notes*.

$$‖O‖ = O + O$$

Rewrite this passage doubling the time values.

Test yourself

Add time signatures and bar lines where necessary.
The first one has been done for you as an example.

Time to check the answers.

PRIMARY TRIADS AND CHORDS

Primary triads are formed on the **tonic – I**
  subdominant – IV
  dominant – V

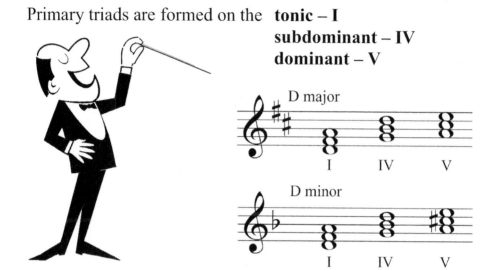

Important

The dominant triad in a minor scale contains the leading note which needs to be raised a semitone / *half step.*

Root, third (3rd) and fifth (5th) refer to the notes of a triad.

Tonic (I), supertonic (II), mediant (III), subdominant (IV), dominant (V), submediant (VI) and leading note (VII) refer to the notes of a scale.

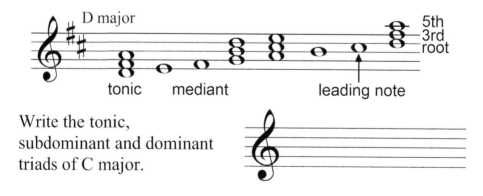

Write the tonic, subdominant and dominant triads of C major.

22

Write the tonic, subdominant and dominant triads of C minor with key signature.

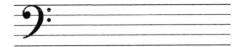

Primary chords

At the level reached in this book you could be asked to name chords that have been formed from the three primary triads. You would not have to write them. You would only have to recognise them. This is easy because the lowest note of the triad – the root – is always at the bottom of the chord in questions at this level.

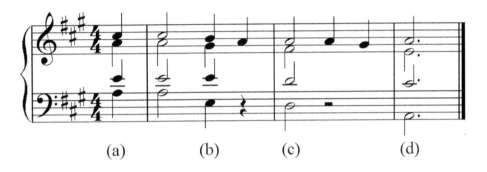

(a)   (b)   (c)   (d)

Name each of the chords (a) to (d) as tonic, subdominant or dominant.

(a) _____

(b) _____

(c) _____

(d) _____

INTERVALS

In my previous books you met major, minor and perfect intervals. Name these. I have done the last one for you.

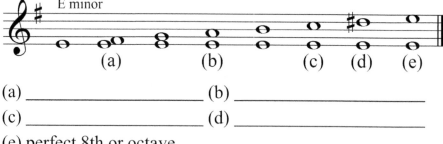

(a) _____ (b) _____

(c) _____ (d) _____

(e) <u>perfect 8th or octave</u> .

You will now meet augmented and diminished intervals.

Augmented means **BIGGER**. An augmented interval is one semitone / *one half step* more than a major interval or a perfect interval.

 A diminished interval is SMALLER. It is one semitone / *one half step* less than a minor interval or one semitone / *one half step* less than a perfect interval.

Handy hints

major + 1 semitone (½ step)	=	**augmented**
perfect + 1 semitone (½ step)	=	**augmented**
minor - 1 semitone (½ step)	=	**diminished**
perfect - 1 semitone (½ step)	=	**diminished**
major - 2 semitones (1 step)	=	**diminished**

Here is a method to take the worry out of intervals so that you can always get the right answer! Follow these instructions to name this interval for example.

Step by Step

1. Decide whether the interval is a 2nd, 3rd, 4th, etc. by counting the letter names. In this example, GABCD = 5 so this is a 5th.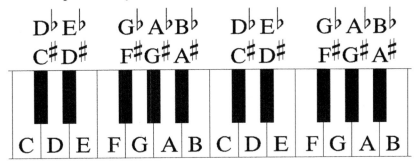

2. Draw a piano keyboard and name the keys.

3. Find the lower note of the interval on the keyboard.

4. Count the semitones / *half steps* by walking your fingers (o) on the keys until you reach the upper note.

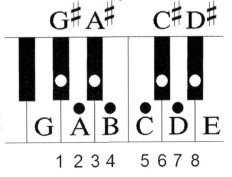

One Final Step

The chart on the next page shows you how many semitones there are in each interval. Look at the chart to name the interval. There are 8 semitones / *8 half steps* in this example so it is an augmented 5th. Remember – 7 semitones / *7 half steps* in a perfect 5th.

25

Interval Chart

Interval		Semitones / *Half steps*
8ve / Perfect	8th	12
Augmented	7th	12
Major	7th	11
Minor	7th	10
Diminished	7th	9
Augmented	6th	10
Major	6th	9
Minor	6th	8
Diminished	6th	7
Augmented	5th	8
Perfect	5th	7
Diminished	5th	6
Augmented	4th	6
Perfect	4th	5
Diminished	4th	4
Augmented	3rd	5
Major	3rd	4
Minor	3rd	3
Diminished	3rd	2
Augmented	2nd	3
Major	2nd	2
Minor	2nd	1
Diminished	2nd	-

Test yourself

Use the interval chart to find the following intervals.

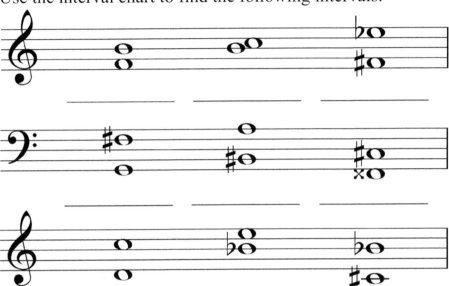

Describe the intervals (a) to (e) in this passage

        (a)   (b) (c)   (d)   (e)

(a) _____

(b) _____

(c) _____

(d) _____

(e) _____

Check your answers

ORNAMENTS

Many candidates 'run away' from facing ornaments. Don't be one of them. The correct playing of ornaments is so important to music that I'm sure you will want to make the effort to understand them. I shall take you through each one very carefully to give you confidence.

For each ornament in this book you will learn to

1. *Recognise* the *sign*.
2. *Write* its name.
3. *Know* how it is *played*.

You will **not** have to write out the notes.

The acciaccatura

It looks like this:- ♪
Acciaccatura is an Italian word meaning 'squeezed in'.

You play it as quickly as possible on the beat, just before you play the main note. We sometimes call the acciaccatura a 'short grace note'.

Note Values

Grace note: = a demisemiquaver
/ *a 32nd note*
Main note: minus a demisemiquaver
/ *a 32nd note*

If the main note is longer than
a crotchet / *a quarter note*:-

If the main note is dotted:-

The appoggiatura

It looks like this ♪ and it has no line through it.

The appoggiatura takes different values, depending on the main note.

Note values

If the main note is not dotted, the grace note is half the value of the main note.

  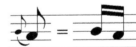

If the main note is dotted,
the grace note is two thirds
the value of the main note.

The double or triple appoggiatura

double 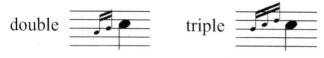 triple

note values

If the main note is not dotted, the grace note is half the value of the main note.

If the main note is dotted, the grace note is two thirds the value of the main note.

So far we have two ornaments:
the acciaccatura (4 letter c's) and
the appoggiatura (2 p's and 2 g's)

Test yourself

Write an acciaccatura before the notes marked with *. Put them a note higher than the given note.

Write an appoggiatura before each note.

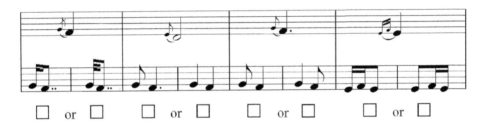

Which do you think is the best way to play the following? Put a tick in the box of your choice.

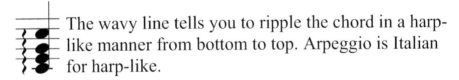

☐ or ☐   ☐ or ☐   ☐ or ☐   ☐ or ☐

The arpeggio

The wavy line tells you to ripple the chord in a harp-like manner from bottom to top. Arpeggio is Italian for harp-like.

When written, the notes take the smallest sensible value and are tied to the notes of the chord.

Each note of the chord is played in turn and held.

The upper mordent

It looks like this

and it is played like this

The main note: a demisemiquaver / *a 32nd note*
The note above: a demisemiquaver / *a 32nd note*
The main note: minus two demisemiquavers / *two 32nd notes.*

When an upper mordent is above a minim / *half note*, add an extra tied crotchet / *quarter note.*

When an upper mordent is above a dotted crotchet / *dotted quarter note,* add an extra tied quaver / *8th note.*

The lower mordent

The main note: a demisemiquaver / *a 32nd note*
The note above: a demisemiquaver / *a 32nd note*
The main note: minus two demisemiquavers / *two 32nd notes.*

It looks like this

and it is played like this

Accidentals and mordents

The accidental is written above the sign with an upper mordent and below the sign with a lower mordent. The middle note is given the accidental indicated.

The upper turn

It looks like this

If **above** a note, it is
played like this.

The note above
The main note
The note below
The main note

Divide the main note into 4 equal notes.

If **after** a note
the main note = half its value
the remainder = 4 equal notes

After a **dotted** note which is a **whole** beat,
the turn = the value of the dot.
For example, in $\frac{6}{8}$ time

After a **dotted** note which is **part** of a beat, a triplet is needed
in the turn. For example, in $\frac{3}{4}$ time

33

Accidentals and turns

Accidentals obey the same rules for turns as for mordents.

If above a turn, accidentals apply to the note above.

If below, accidentals apply to the note below.

Test yourself

Tick the box showing the best way to play these ornaments.

☐   or   ☐   ☐   or   ☐

☐   or   ☐   ☐   or   ☐

☐   or   ☐

The trill or shake

It looks like this tr or tr ᴧᴧᴧᴧ
It is played with the main note and the note above.
With early composers, start a trill on the note above.

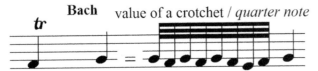

Use semiquavers / *16th notes* for fast pieces and
demisemiquavers / *32nd notes* for slower pieces.

If a trill begins with an acciaccatura, start on the note above.

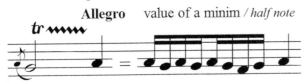

With modern composers, start a trill on the main note.

Avoid repeated notes at the beginning or the end of a trill. If
this means adding an extra note, you will need a triplet before
the last two notes of the trill (see above).

Grace notes are included in the trill.

Ready to test yourself? Turn over.

35

Test yourself

Put a tick / *check mark* in the box showing the best way to play these trills or shakes.

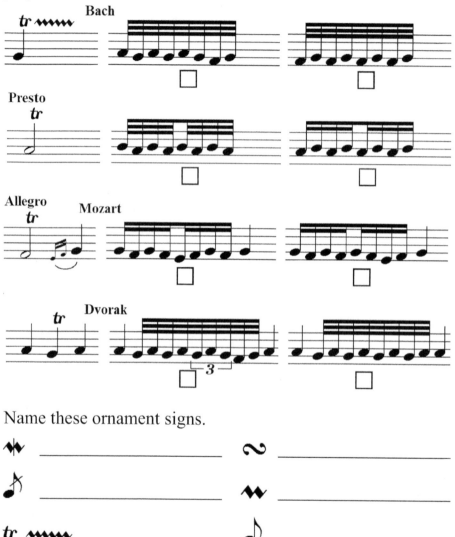

Name these ornament signs.

Write the signs for the ornaments

upper turn

trill or shake

lower mordent

appoggiatura

upper mordent

acciaccatura.

Time to check your answers.

37

WORDS AND RHYTHM

In my Music Theory is Fun Book 3 you met four-bar
rhythms. A musical phrase is often four bars in length. In this
book we shall look at writing a rhythm to words. Here is an
example:-

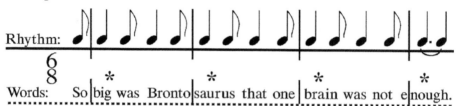

Rhythm:

$\frac{6}{8}$

Words: So big was Bronto saurus that one brain was not enough.

- I put bar lines in front of important syllables (see *)
- I chose a time $\frac{6}{8}$ signature since it combines duple time
  and the possibility of dividing a beat into 3.
- I wrote separate notes for each syllable.

Test yourself

Compose rhythms for the following words.

    Give thought, now, to the dinosaurs,
    Whom no-one fears today.

rhythm _____

words ....

rhythm _____

words ....

Whenever you look at moon and stars,
Whenever the wind is wild.

rhythm _____

words ....

rhythm _____

words ....

Write four-bar rhythms in the times given. Begin with an anacrusis before bar 1. You met the anacrusis in Book 3.

$\frac{4}{4}$ _____

_____

$\frac{6}{8}$ _____

_____

Hurry! Take me to the next topic!

INSTRUMENTS OF THE ORCHESTRA

Instrument	treble	alto	tenor	bass
violin	●			
viola		●		
cello	(●)		(●)	●
double bass				●
flute	●			
oboe	●			
bassoon			(●)	●
clarinet	●			
trumpet	●			
horn	●			●
trombone			(●)	●
tuba				●

(●) this clef is sometimes used. Knowledge of the tenor clef is not expected at this level.

A note about notes
String instruments can play more than one note at a time - sometimes two, three or even four notes. Wind instruments can play only one note at a time.

The string family

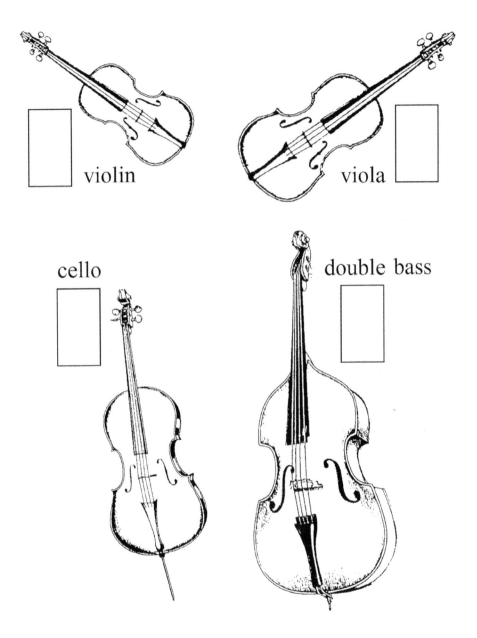

violin

viola

cello

double bass

In each box draw the main clef for the instrument.

The woodwind family

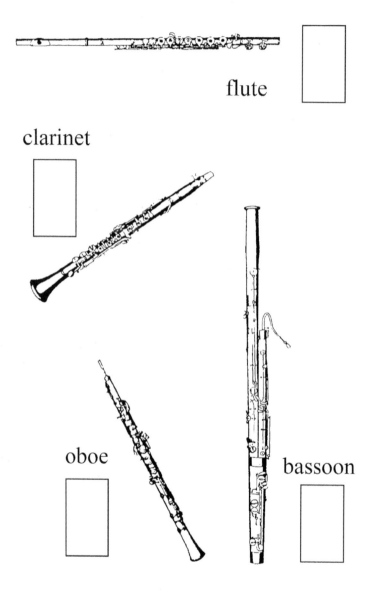

flute

clarinet

oboe

bassoon

In each box draw the main clef for the instrument.

The brass family

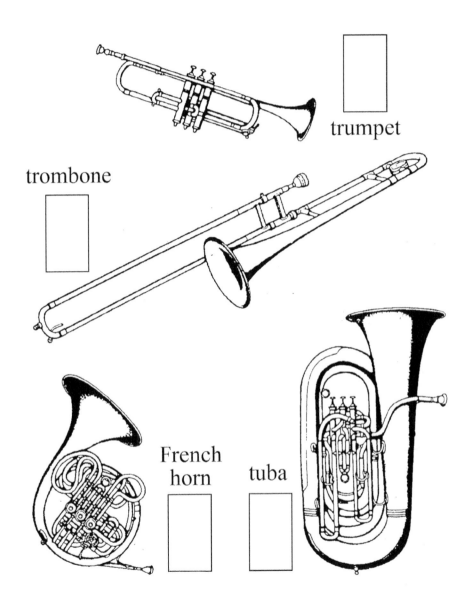

trumpet

trombone

French horn

tuba

In each box draw the main clef for the instrument.

The percussion family

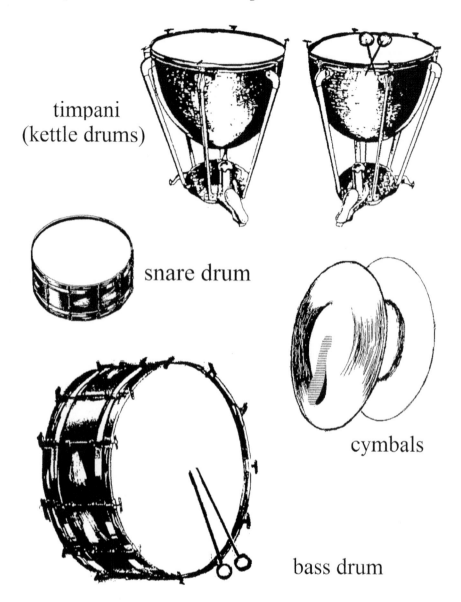

timpani
(kettle drums)

snare drum

cymbals

bass drum

Some members of the percussion family contribute to the
rhythm and dynamics of a piece of music. Others can play
notes of varying pitch. We shall look more closely at this
family in Book 5.

Performance Directions

Brass and string instruments can use a mute to play quietly.

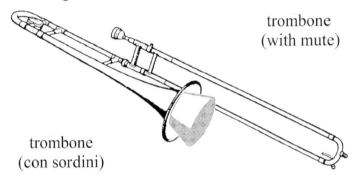

trombone
(with mute)

trombone
(con sordini)

The term **senza sordini** tells you to play without a mute.

To a violinist, ⌐ means 'down' bow and V means 'up' bow.   Here are some other directions for string players:

play on the G string	**sul G**
play near the bridge	**sul ponticello**
pluck the strings	**pizzicato**
play with the bow	**arco**

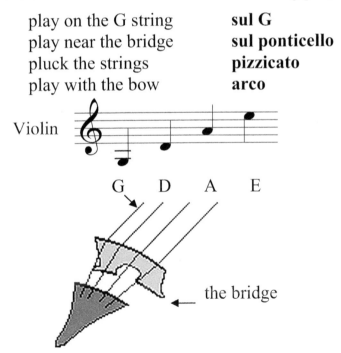

Violin

G   D   A   E

the bridge

Test yourself

Name the family for each instrument.

1. violin   _____

2. oboe   _____

3. trombone   _____

4. bassoon   _____

5. clarinet   _____

6. tuba   _____

7. timpani   _____

Name the main clef for each instrument.

8. cello   _____

9. clarinet   _____

10. flute   _____

11. trumpet   _____

12. tuba   _____

13. viola   _____

14. French horn   _____

Check your answers.

PUZZLES

QUIZZES

TESTS

Fun Page

Draw a string for each balloon.

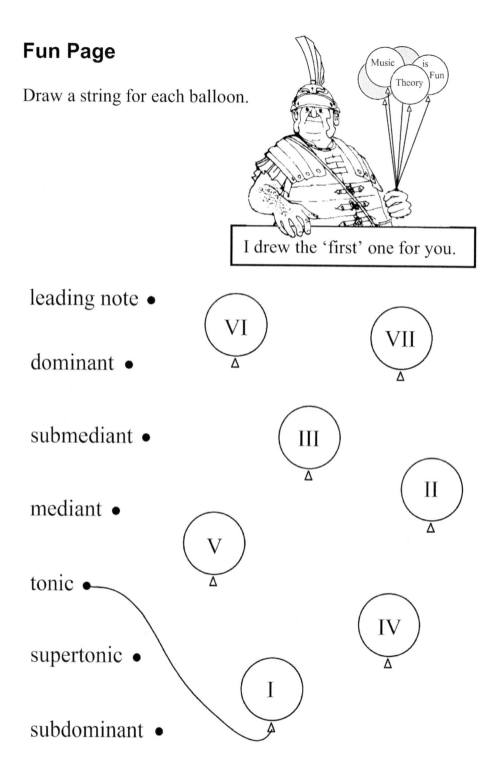

I drew the 'first' one for you.

leading note •

dominant •

submediant •

mediant •

tonic •

supertonic •

subdominant •

48

Anagrams

caratacacuci

[ ]

Clue: This ornament is played as quickly as possible on the beat and just before the main note.

ograpige

[ ]

Clue: This wavy line means ripple the chord like on a harp.

frecept hofurt

[ ]

Clue: This is an interval of 5 semitones / *5 half steps.*

rajmo veenths

[ ]

Clue: This is an interval of 11 semitones / *11 half steps.*

hiddinmeis

[ ]

Clue: These intervals are 1 semitone / *1 half step* less than a minor interval.

tombudanins

[ ]

Clue: This is also called chord IV.

Crossword

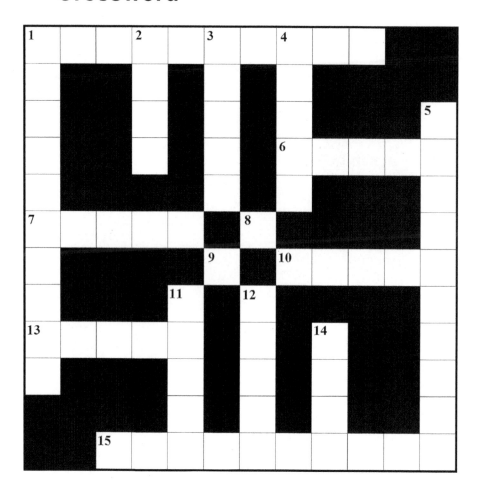

Across

1 hammered out

6 sadly

7 hold back [ritenuto]

8 minor key with 4 flats

9 major key with 5 sharps

10 sweetly

13 below

15 sighing

Down

1 mysteriously

2 very

3 slowly

4 animated, lively

5 loud then immediately soft

11 less

12 as if, resembling

14 in the style of

Answers?

Yes. Ready to check?

Musical terms word search

I	B	A	S	O	P	R	A	E	S
A	R	W	O	U	K	A	C	Y	A
X	A	E	T	X	I	O	R	B	N
Y	L	Q	T	G	L	Y	Q	V	S
M	E	N	O	E	L	U	I	S	N
E	N	C	V	G	N	P	Z	K	I
Q	T	K	B	G	I	U	S	T	O
Y	I	F	V	F	V	O	Q	X	M
O	R	O	N	O	S	B	G	I	G
H	B	X	B	V	I	F	P	E	U

Meaning   **Musical term**

lively   vif _____

slow down   _____

held back   _____

exact, proper _____

with rich tone _____

without   _____

above   _____

below   _____

swift   _____

less   _____

little   _____

Quiz 1

Put a tick / *check mark* (✓) for the correct answer.

1. marcato
- ☐ majestically
- ☐ in a military style
- ☐ hammered out
- ☐ marked, accented

2. sadly
- ☐ dolente
- ☐ dolce
- ☐ dolore
- ☐ delicato

3. with a strong accent
- ☐ forte
- ☐ fortissimo
- ☐ forzando
- ☐ pesante

4. ∾
- ☐ upper turn
- ☐ upper mordent
- ☐ lower mordent
- ☐ shake

5. with vigour
- ☐ con anima
- ☐ con brio
- ☐ con moto
- ☐ con spirito

6. meno
- ☐ less
- ☐ more
- ☐ moderately
- ☐ much

7. from the beginning
- ☐ dal segno
- ☐ a tempo
- ☐ da capo
- ☐ prima volta

8.
- ☐ short, detached
- ☐ accent the note
- ☐ staccatissimo
- ☐ staccato

Quiz 2

Do you know these orchestral instruments? Write in the box the name of the instrument being played.

Handy hints for tests

This section is for you to practise the different types of questions you could have in a test or an exam.

The questions could be on any topic covered in this book and in Music Theory is Fun Books 1, 2 and 3.

Revise each topic in this book thoroughly.

Don't forget to study musical terms and signs – they are **always** included.

Practice
makes perfect !

If you have worked through this book carefully and understood each topic, this will be an easy task for you.

Practice
makes perfect !

Before you begin any test, write out your key signature chart (see page 7). Always refer to the chart when tackling questions that require you to know a key signature.

Test 1

1. Name this interval.

major 7th ☐   augmented 6th ☐   diminished 7th ☐

2. Smorzando means

gradually slower ☐   dying away ☐   tearfully ☐

3. Which minor key has 5 sharps in its key signature?

F ☐   C ☐   G♯ ☐

4. Which minor key has 4 flats in its key signature?

F ☐   C ☐   B ☐

5. Which note is the mediant in this minor key?

G ☐   A ☐   D ☐

6. This note is

lowered one semitone / *one half step* ☐
lowered one tone / *one whole step* ☐
raised one semitone / *one half step* ☐

7. Which is the correct time signature for this bar?

$\frac{3}{8}$ ☐ $\frac{5}{8}$ ☐ $\frac{5}{4}$ ☐

8. How many semiquavers / *16th notes* are there in this note?

5 ☐   6 ☐   7 ☐

Test 2

1. Put a Roman numeral under each note in this D major
   scale.

   ___ ___ ___ ___ ___ ___ ___ ___

2. How many quavers / *8th notes* are there in these notes?

   ___ ___ ___ ___

3. Name these ornament signs.

   (a) 𝅘 _____

   (b) ∿ _____

   (c) 𝅘 _____

   (d) *tr*∿∿∿ _____

   (e) ♪ _____

4. What does this metronome setting mean? ♩ = **80**

   _____

5. Write the chromatic scale of G major in the treble clef
   ascending in semibreves / *whole notes* with key
   signature.

Test 3

1. Name the four main families of orchestral instruments.

_____   _____

_____   _____

2. What is the meaning of

(a) sul ponticello _____

(b) pizzicato _____

(c) arco _____

3. (a) What is the meaning of senza sordini?

_____

   (b) Name an instrument that might have this direction.

_____

4. Write in semibreves / *whole notes* the scale of D♭ major ascending in the treble clef with key signature.

5. Write in semibreves / *whole notes* the scale of G♯ melodic minor descending in the bass clef without key signature.

Test 4

1. Write a note above the given note to form the named melodic intervals.

   (a) augmented 4th   (b) diminished 7th.

2. Put accidentals in front of the notes that need them to make the scale of C melodic minor. Do not use a key signature.

3. Write the scale of G♯ harmonic minor ascending in minims / *half notes* using the bass clef. Do not put a key signature. Add any necessary accidentals.

4. **patetico** means

   dying away   ☐

   with feeling   ☐

   tearfully   ☐

   sadly   ☐

5. ♪ is the sign for

   upper mordent   ☐

   appoggiatura   ☐

   acciaccatura   ☐

   trill   ☐

Test 5

1. Name the family for each instrument.

   oboe _____

   cello _____

   trumpet _____

   timpani _____

2. Write the scale of F melodic minor in the bass clef ascending in minims / *half notes* with key signature.

3. Write the letter names of the notes on the white keys.

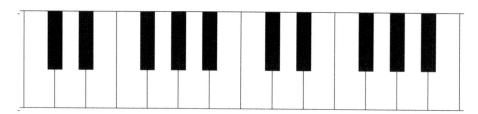

4. **Write above the black keys the letter names of (a) the flats and (b) the sharps.**

   (a) — —   — — — (b) — —   — — —

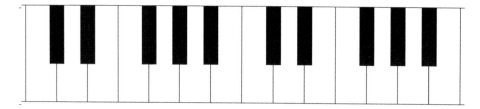

Test 6

1. Write these alto clef notes at the same pitch in the treble clef.

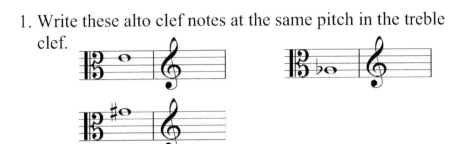

2. Write the chromatic scale beginning on A♭ with key signature ascending in semibreves / *whole notes* using the treble clef. Remember the accidentals.

3. Write the chromatic scale beginning on D without key signature ascending in semibreves / *whole notes* using the alto clef. Put in all necessary accidentals.

4. Describe each of these harmonic intervals fully e.g. major 3rd, perfect 4th.

      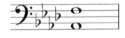

_____   _____   _____

5. Name these notes.

____   ____   ____

Test 7

1. Find the mistakes in this piece of music and then write it out correctly on the stave below.

2. Write the tonic, subdominant and dominant triads of F major in the treble clef with key signature.

4. Write the tonic, subdominant and dominant triads of F minor in the treble clef with key signature.

5. Compose rhythms to these words from a poem by Robert Frost.
   The woods are lovely, dark and deep
   But I have promises to keep
   Begin with an anacrusis. Add a time signature.

rhythm _____

words _____

rhythm _____

words _____

Test 8

1. Give the meaning of Patetico. _____

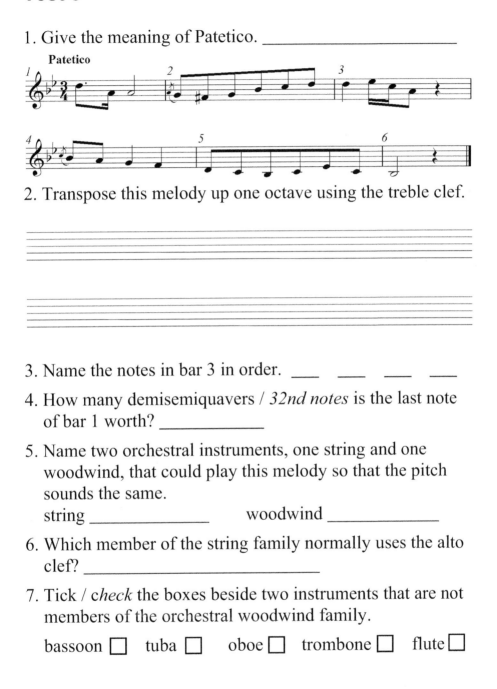

2. Transpose this melody up one octave using the treble clef.

3. Name the notes in bar 3 in order. ___ ___ ___ ___

4. How many demisemiquavers / *32nd notes* is the last note of bar 1 worth? _____

5. Name two orchestral instruments, one string and one woodwind, that could play this melody so that the pitch sounds the same.
   string _____   woodwind _____

6. Which member of the string family normally uses the alto clef? _____

7. Tick / *check* the boxes beside two instruments that are not members of the orchestral woodwind family.

   bassoon ☐   tuba ☐   oboe ☐   trombone ☐   flute ☐

Test 9

Look at the following piece of music and answer the questions that follow.

1. Add a key signature in the bass clef and add a time signature in the treble and bass clefs.

2. Copy the treble part in bar 1 and mark the beats with a stroke (|) between each beat.

3. What is the Italian word for the ornament (♪) at the beginning of bar 2 and what does it mean? Is it played quickly or slowly?

4. Give the meaning of ♩ = 120

5. Name the notes in the last chord in the treble clef in bar 2.

   _____   _____

6. Name the number and type of interval between the notes in the last chord in the treble clef in bar 2.

   number _____   type _____

64

Test 10

Look at this melody and then answer the questions below.

1. Add the time signature of this melody in the correct place.

2. Describe the time signature as simple, compound duple, triple or quadruple. _____

3. What is the key of the piece? _____

4. Give the letter names of the first three notes in bar 1.

   _____   _____   _____

5. Give the letter name of the highest note in the melody.

   _____

6. Name the ornaments in bars 3 & 4. _____

7. Look at bar 5 then give the meaning of

   (a) ⌒ _____

   (b) ⌢ _____

8. How should the notes in bar 4 be played?

   _____

MUSICAL TERMS AND SIGNS

Musical terms

A (à) - at, to, by, for, in the style of
Accelerando - becoming gradually faster
Adagietto - rather slow
Adagio - slow, leisurely
Adagissimo - very slow
Affetuoso - tenderly
Affrettando - hurrying
Agitato - agitated
Alla - in the style of
Alla marcia - in the style of a march
Alla polacca - in the style of a Polonaise
Allargando - broadening out
Allegretto - slightly slower than allegro
Allegro - lively, reasonably fast
Allegro assai - very quick
Amabile - amiable, pleasant
Andante - at a walking pace
Andantino - a little slower or a little faster than andante
Animato - lively, animated
Animé - animated, lively
Appassionata - with passion
Assai - very
Assez - enough, sufficiently
Attacca - go on immediately
A tempo - resume the normal speed
Avec - with
Bravura - with boldness and spirit
Brillante - sparkling, brilliant
Cantabile - in a singing style
Cantando - in a singing style
Cédez - yield, relax the speed
Col; Con - with

Con anima - with deep feeling - soul
Con brio - with vigour
Con moto - with movement
Con spirito - with spirit, life, energy
Crescendo [cresc.] - gradually louder
Da capo [D.C.] - from the beginning
Dal segno [D.S.] - repeat from the sign
Deciso - with determination
Decrescendo [decresc.] - gradually softer
Delicato - delicately
Diminuendo [dim.] - gradually softer
Dolce - sweetly
Dolcissimo - very sweetly
Dolente - sadly
Dolore - grief, sorrow
Doppio - double
Doppio movimento - double the speed
Douce - sweet
En dehors - prominent
Energico - with energy
Espressione - expression
Espressivo [Espress., Espr.] - with expression, feeling
Et - and
Facile - easy
Fortepiano [*fp*] - loud, then immediately soft
Fine - the end
Forte [*f*] - loud
Fortissimo [*ff*] - very loud
Forza - force, power
Forzando [*fz*] - with a strong accent
Fuoco - fire
Furioso - furiously
Giocoso - merry
Giusto - exact, proper

Grandioso - in a grand manner
Grave - very slow
Grazioso - gracefully
Lacrimoso - tearfully
Largamente - in a broad style
Larghetto - faster than largo
Largo - slow & stately, broad
Legatissimo - as smoothly as possible
Legato - smoothly
Légèrement - lightly
Leggiero - lightly
Lent - slow
Lento - slowly
L'Istesso - the same
Ma - but
Ma non troppo - but not too much
Maestoso - majestically
Mais - but
Marcato - strong accent
Martellato - hammered out
Marziale - in a military style
Meno - less
Meno mosso - less movement
Mesto - sadly
Mezzo forte [*mf*] - moderately loud
Mezzo piano [*mp*] - moderately soft
Misterioso - mysteriously
Moderato - at a moderate pace
Modéré - at a moderate speed
Moins - less
Molto - much
Morendo - dying away
Mosso - movement
Moto - movement

Movimento - movement
Niente - nothing
Nobilmente - nobly
Non - not
Non tanto - not so much
Non troppo - not too much
Parlando - in a speaking manner
Parlante - in a speaking manner
Pastorale - in a pastoral style
Patetico - with feeling
Perdendosi - dying away
Pesante - heavily
Peu - little
Pianissimo [*pp*] - very soft
Piano [*p*] - soft
Piu - more
Pizzicato [pizz.] - plucked
Plus - more
Poco a poco - little by little
Possibile - possible
    Presto possibile - as fast as possible
Presser - hurry
    En pressant - hurrying on
Prestissimo - as fast as possible
Presto - very quick
Quasi - as if, resembling
Ralentir - slow down
Rallentando [rall.] - becoming gradually slower
Retenu - held back
    En retenant - holding back
Risoluto - boldly
Ritardando [ritard. rit.] - gradually slower
Ritenuto [riten. rit.] - hold back, slower at once
Ritmico - rhythmically

Sans - without
Scherzando - playfully
Scherzo - a joke
Semplice - simple
Sempre - always
Senza - without
Sforzando [*sf*, *sfz*] - with a sudden accent
Simile [Sim.] - in the same way
Slargando - gradually slower
Slentando - gradually slower
Smorzando - dying away
Sonoro - with rich tone
Sopra - above
Sospirando - sighing
Sostenuto - sustained
Sotto - below
Sotto voce - in an undertone
Spiritoso - lively, animated
Staccatissimo - very detached
Staccato - short, detached
Stringendo - gradually faster
Subito - suddenly
Tanto - so much
Tempo - speed, time
Tempo comodo - at a comfortable speed
Tempo primo - resume the original speed
Tempo rubato - with some freedom of time
Tenuto - held on
Tranquillo - quietly
Très - very
Triste, Tristamente - sad, sorrowful
Troppo - too much
Tutti - all
Veloce - swift

Vibrato - vibrating
Vif - lively
Vite - quick
Vivace, Vivo - lively, quick
Vivacissimo - very lively
Voce - voice
Volta - time
    Prima volta - first time
    Seconda volta - second time
Volti subito [V.S.] - turn the page quickly

Common Alternative Terms

measure		bar
double whole note		*breve*
whole note		semibreve
half note		minim
quarter note		crotchet
eighth note (8th)		quaver
sixteenth note (*16th*)		semiquaver
thirty-second note (32nd)		demisemiquaver
whole step		tone
half step		semitone

73

Musical signs and symbols

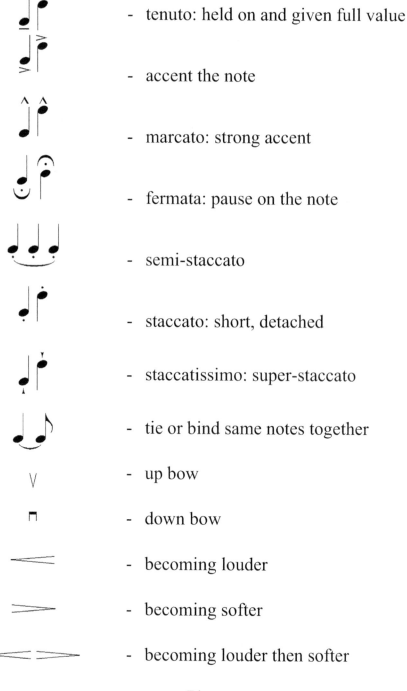

- tenuto: held on and given full value

- accent the note

- marcato: strong accent

- fermata: pause on the note

- semi-staccato

- staccato: short, detached

- staccatissimo: super-staccato

- tie or bind same notes together

- up bow

- down bow

- becoming louder

- becoming softer

- becoming louder then softer

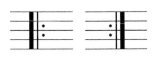 - start repeat and end repeat

 - 60 crotchet/ *quarter note* beats in a minute

 - slurs: play the group of notes smoothly

 - play an octave higher

 - play an octave lower

 - acciaccatura, and appoggiatura

 - flat, natural and sharp

 - double flat and double sharp

- turn and inverted turn

- upper mordent and lower mordent

- trill or shake

 - arpeggio (harp-like)

alto clef   treble clef   bass clef

Printed in Great Britain
by Amazon

80907172R00047